THE INSPIRATION BOOK

Thoughts and Stories for Greater Living

by
TIM GAITHER

Awaken Publishing
Houston, Texas

The Inspiration Book
©1996 Awaken Publishing

ISBN 1-887918-02-7

Awaken Publishing

Printed in cooperation with
Brockton Publishing
8326 Southwest Freeway
Houston, Texas 77074
1-800-968-7065

Graphic Design by Mark Thogerson

∞ DEDICATION PAGE ∞

Mom & Dad who taught me values
Dale Carnegie who was my first inspiration
Zig Zigler who showed me the way to the top
Tony Robbins who helped awaken my giant within
George Doyen who inspired me to write
Jackie Greer who exemplifies love
Bill Ferguson who taught me to live in love
Dr. Jim Moore who inspires me with his sermons
Dr. John Gray who helped me understand the sexes
George Bush who showed me how to make a difference
Colin Powell for being an American hero

THANKS AND APPRECIATION TO ALL THESE WHO HELPED MAKE THIS BOOK A REALITY!

Byron Barnes	Brocky Brown
Bill Ferguson	Donna Fisher
Noreen Foley	Alita Gail
Doreen Gaither	Lynette Gordan
Kim Gray	Susan Haines
Nancy Hawthorne	Michelle Herring
Darlene Love	Tina Meyer
Lee McKenzie	Joan Thompson
Russell Treat	Sandy Vilas
Joe Vitale	Christine Witte

∞ TABLE OF CONTENTS ∞

Introduction 7

Self and Others 9

Motivation and Desire 25

Happiness and Peace 37

Success and Failure 51

Mental, Physical and spiritual 67

Balance and Growth 81

Problems and Solutions 91

Love and Fear 101

My Formula for a Rich and Fulfilling Life 114

Ending Note 115

Sources of My Inspiration 116

"The ideas I stand for are not mine. I borrowed them from Socrates. I swiped them from Chesterfield. I stole them from Jesus. And I put them in a book. If you don't like their rules, whose would you use?" - DALE CARNEGIE

"Let us not come to the end of our lives with the realization that we have not yet lived." - ANONYMOUS

"A hundred times every day I remind myself that my inner and outer life are based on the labors of other men, living and dead, and that I must exert myself in order to give in the same measure as I have received and am still receiving." - ALBERT EINSTEIN

"When living and learning seem to reach a plateau, it is time to seek your next challenge" - TIM GAITHER

Following the pages of this introduction are thoughts and stories which literally display the essence of living. You will come away from this book with an increased awareness of living in such a way that the experience of love, joy and peace are more commonplace. I believe that this book was truly inspired and now try to explain how it came about.

One night I found myself tossing and turning. I tried to sleep, but could only lay there restless. Finally, at 2:00 a.m., I got up and walked around the house. It was peaceful and very still as I looked outside through the windows. I went down the stairs and tried to relax, but something inside would not let me rest. I settled down at the breakfast table with a notepad and began to jot down ideas which seemed to flow into my mind. I had read hundreds of books on success, love, relationships, God and many other areas of life. I had also listened to numerous tapes and attended seminars dealing with both success and relationship development. It seemed that the key points and ideas of all of those books and my experiences were poring out of me. In the peace of the night I felt as if I were hearing the whispers of angels guiding me to write down the aspects of a fulfilling life.

By the time the sun was coming up, I had composed a list of over 100 ideas about what seemed true of life. All of these ideas have evolved by those who have preceded me and have in some way left their mark for others in the literature that they have produced. How much easier my life could have been, had I read and understood these ideas earlier.

I invite you to take your time and simply enjoy the stories within this book. I provide eight different sections which cover the areas essential to obtaining a fulfilling life: self and others; motivation and desire; happiness and peace; success and failure; mental, physical and spiritual; balance and growth; problems and solutions; love and fear. Within each section I have included a few ideas and then, on the opposite page, present a story which illustrates what the ideas represent.

I will let you decide whether this book is simply a subconscious flow of everything I have read and heard or whether it truly was an inspiration.

∞ SELF AND OTHERS ∞

This section takes a look at the outcome of our lives when we focus on our selves and when we focus on others. It seems that when we focus only on what we want and need, we never have enough to make us happy. I could always use a nicer car. I could always use some nicer clothes. I could always use some more friends, etc. However, when I focus on what others need and how I can help them, something else begins to take place. I guess my car is okay after all. Maybe someone could use the sportcoat I haven't worn in years. I enjoy having friends who appreciate my help. As you can see, a good start to a fulfilling life is to focus on others instead of only yourself.

The greatest gift we can give another is to help each person see within what their gift to the world is.

To realize that others are a reflection of ourselves is the beginning of knowing ourselves.

"You are always good enough when you help others feel good enough." - ZIG ZIGLER

Andrew Carnegie is known for his multi-million dollar steel empire. He at one time had more millionaires working for him than anyone. He was interviewed about his success and how he was able to attract so many millionaires. He explained that they were not millionaires when he found them. Carnegie said that he was able to recognize people with special skills and talents and was able to develop them. He looked at people like a gold mine. Most people just saw the dirt on the outside. However, he believed that to get to the gold, you often need to move some dirt aside. Everyone has their gold inside. What is your gold? When dealing with people, do you focus on the dirt or the gold? Obviously Andrew Carnegie knew what to focus on with others.

*Life should be a game
to see who can out serve who.*

*Those who die
giving away the most toys win.*

*Focus on yourself and the world becomes smaller,
focus on others and the world becomes greater.*

Mother Teresa would be a strong contender in the game of trying to out serve others and give away the most toys! What can we learn from her example? She actually started her career early in life by serving wealthy families in India by taking care of their children. She perhaps gained some satisfaction from helping others grow and have a comfortable lifestyle. It was not until she saw a helpless poor person lying down on the streets of India, and then bent down to try to comfort the tormented soul who was too weak to even keep the bugs off of them, that Mother Teresa discovered her purpose and joy in life. By helping the poor and destitute of the world minimize their agony and suffering, Mother Teresa discovered an incredible peace and love that exudes from her everywhere she goes. How can you serve the world? Where can you begin to make a difference? When you answer these questions, you will be on your way to finding your purpose.

*Develop your dreams and you create passion,
develop the dreams of others and you create heaven.*

*Education is the opportunity of each man to
recognize his equality with each other.*

*You can tell the greatness of big men by
how they treat little men.*

This is a story of a mother and her son. Her son was only five when a tremendous event happened. He had just begun taking piano lessons. His mother thought that it would be very inspirational and encouraging to take him to see one of the greatest pianists of the day who was performing at the concert hall. It would be a rare opportunity for them to see a live piano performance of tremendous caliber. She was able to get some tickets which were only a couple of rows back. They arrived early enough to get settled in their seats and for her to get some refreshments. While she was away, the little boy became enchanted by the huge, beautiful, shiny, grand piano in front of him on the stage. When she got back to her seat, he was gone. Then, to the notes of 'Twinkle Twinkle Little Star', she saw her son in front of the entire concert hall playing on the piano. But, before she could pass out, the pianist who was to perform stepped up next to her son and began to add beautiful music coinciding with her son. The crowd erupted in applause after they stopped and the great pianist told the little man to follow his dream. What would it be like if your hero encouraged you? Whose hero are you? Who can you encourage?

*"Everyone in some way is superior to you,
in that you should learn from them"* - HENRY DAVID THOREAU

*Once you begin to recognize the greatness in each person,
the world begins to recognize the greatness in you.*

*To minimize prejudice against yourself,
minimize prejudice against others.*

Here is an example that clearly demonstrates that we can learn something from everyone we meet, regardless of their apparent limitations. The Special Olympics is an event in which handicapped children compete in athletic games much like those of the real Olympics. During the games in Seattle, Washington, there was an event which revealed some real champions. During a specific race, nine mentally challenged children were at their starting positions waiting for the gun to sound. They had practiced time and time again. They had gained much pride and satisfaction to make it to the National finals. Now they were about to compete for a gold medal! Bang! They were off. One boy got off to a great start. But in his excitement, he tripped, and fell to the ground. The crowd stood in amazement as a couple of the kids stopped to help, until they were joined by all the runners who got the boy up and helped him finish the race with them. As the group finished, the crowd gave a standing ovation. Obviously, these runners valued each other more than a gold medal. Maybe there's a lesson for all of us here somewhere.

*Only a fool judges others without all the information—
since we never have all the information—
should we ever judge others?*

*A man should no more hate another man
any more than his own head hate his heart.*

*If the more we get to know someone,
the less credit we give them,
how much credit can we give ourselves?*

"I don't know what your destiny will be, but one thing I do know; the only ones among you who will be really happy are those who will have sought and found how to serve." - ALBERT SCHWEITZER

"He who wishes to secure the good of others has already secured his own."

"When you see a worthy person, endeavor to emulate him, when you see an unworthy person, then examine your inner self." - CONFUCIUS

"You can't hold a man down without staying down with him." - BOOKER T. WASHINGTON

*Become what
you want to attract.*

*Never demand of others what
you would not demand of yourself.*

*"People don't care how much you know,
until they know how much you care."* - ZIG ZIGLER

Mahatma Gandhi has been acclaimed as one of the great leaders of the 20th century. Here is an example of a man who set a great example to influence others to be their best. His native country of India was being torn apart in hatred between Moslem and Hindu actions. Gandhi saw each and every man as a brother and a part of God. He stated that "we must become the change we want to see in the world." By practicing peaceful resistance, Gandhi succeeded against Britain, one of the most powerful governments of the day. He helped calm the torment between the two religious factions. Gandhi never asked his fellow man to do anything which he would not do. More importantly, with his steadfast love and understanding, he helped a large part of mankind discover more about their similarities than their differences. Gandhi proved that the combination of love and understanding toward others results in a peace for yourself and the world in which you live.

*People trust more easily those
who are like themselves.*

*The best way to influence others is to give
credit to them and accept responsibility for yourself.*

*To appreciate yourself begins with
finding ways you can help others.*

Benjamin Franklin is known as one of America's greatest diplomats. When asked about some of the attributes that contributed to his success, Franklin stated, "I speak ill of no man, and speak all the good I know of every man." He never tired of learning and developing good habits. He taught himself the value of taking responsibility for his actions and the importance of serving mankind. Through his scientific experiments and his inquisitive mind, Franklin developed inventions which benefitted everyone. Although most famous for his experiments regarding electricity, Franklin also developed bifocal glasses to help those with poor vision continue to learn through reading. He also was a very successful diplomat to France during the American Revolution. By learning the French language and customs, Franklin was able to better earn the trust and admiration of the French to support Americans. In what ways can you develop to better serve others? Who do you need to give credit to for your life being better? Where do you need to take responsibility?

∞ Motivation and Desire ∞

If you had all of the motivation and desire in the world, what could you achieve? What can we do in life to increase our motivation? What would we do in life if we knew we would not fail? Focussing our energy and thoughts on what we want in life is a key to increasing motivation and desire. We must discover what we want in life and why we seek it. I believe that if we are given a desire, we are also given the ability to make that desire come true. However, most people seem to have lost their motivation and desire. Where did it go? How can we get it back? Most likely, a few setbacks have lead us to believe in false limitations. This section will explore ways of removing those limitations.

*Enthusiasm comes from the ability to dream,
and the ability to make those dreams come true.*

*The majority of your effort will be your first step,
the majority of your memories will be in your last steps,
the majority of your joy should be in all the steps in between.*

There is no purpose for a man who believes in nothing.

The key obstacle squelching much of our desire and motivation is FEAR. FEAR stands for False Evidence Appearing Real. Franklin D. Roosevelt stated it best "There is nothing to fear but fear itself." Fear is learned from unpleasant experiences. However, fear is only supposed to teach us 'how not' to do something, instead of not to do it at all. When you fall off a bike and scrape your knee, you learn a lesson on how not to ride a bike. Then you get back on until you learn how. Only then does your fear diminish and your desire and motivation to ride a bike increase. A good example of having false limitations is circus elephants. When an elephant is young, it is chained to a steel post driven into the ground to keep the elephant in place. After a few weeks, a rope replaces the chain. Eventually a grown elephant is kept in place by a rope and a wooden stake. Because the elephant learned that it could not budge the steel post earlier, it never tries to break loose from the simple wooden stake. What wooden stake is holding you back? What other false limitations have you held on to?

Live your life as if the whole world depended on you; someday, in some way, you may discover that it actually did.

A man can't appreciate his labors unless he sees something grow from them.

What is the reason for man's existence if not for the betterment of the world?

In the movie "It's A Wonderful Life," George Bailey lives his life to the very best he knows how. He tends to put others first, and does a good job serving his community. When his business is threatened with bankruptcy and life throws him a few curves on top of everything, he contemplates throwing his life away. He doesn't see everything that has happened from his efforts. He becomes focussed only on his problems. An angel shows up and shows George what the world would have been without him. His younger brother Harry drowns because George was not there to save him. A troop ship goes down because Harry was not there to save it from an enemy plane. His hometown, Bedford Falls, becomes a shanty town because George was not there to provide good housing for the community. His wife, Mary, was a spinster because he was not there to love her. His four children would never have been. Once George realized how rich his life was, he became a new man full of motivation and desire to keep living a full life. What difference have you made in your part of the world? Maybe you need to live your life as if the world needs you!

A motto for life- "What ever it takes... and then some!"

It is better to reach for the heavens and end up with a few stars than to reach for the ground and end up with dirt.

What would you do if you knew that you could not fail- that is your dream.

Christopher Columbus is most known for his discovery of the "New World." However, had he not given "what ever it takes, and then some" to his pursuit, the "New World" may have waited a little longer. Columbus was a mathematician and made calculations about how long it would take to reach the "New World." Once at sea, and beyond the time and distance calculated to reach his destination, Columbus had a big decision to make. He had already done 'what ever it took' to reach his goal... but he had still not attained his goal. He could either return home or give it the 'and then some.' By continuing on, Columbus did indeed discover the "New World." By pushing after his goal with the belief that he would not fail, Columbus was able to give it the extra effort to accomplish his dream. What is it going to take to reach your dreams?

*God gave man the ability to dream,
and the ability to make those dreams come true.*

*Discover your heros,
and then become someone else's hero.*

*To discover your purpose is to know the
essence and moving force of your life.*

Here is a story of what can happen in America. A boy was born in 1937. He spent his earliest years in Harlem and later in South Bronx. He grew up in an environment that most would say offered little chance of living the American Dream. However, this boy had the support of two loving parents and lived in an area where many cultures melted into one. He grew up with belief in himself and a desire to make things happen. He was one of the few to go to college from his area in 1954. While in school, he developed a passion for military life. He had the desire to do the best he could and to serve his country. He experienced racism in the south while at Fort Benning, Georgia and adversity while serving in Vietnam. Even so, his desire for leadership never diminished. In September 1990 this man showed that he was the best by leading joint forces in the Gulf War to victory. Colin Powell reflects all that is possible when a person lives out their God given desire to make their mark on the World. What desire or dream do you have? What skills and talents have you been given to make your dream come true?

"You must become the example of what you want to see in the world." - MAHATMA GANDHI

With knowledge, as with any gift, comes the responsibility to use it to serve.

The lower man's focus on his needs are, the more dangerous he becomes.

Our initial experience with anything is usually the greatest; if you fear something, simply gain more experience with it and the fear will fade.

"I'm a great believer in luck, and I find the harder I work, the more I have of it." - THOMAS JEFFERSON

"The average person puts only 25% of his energy and ability into his work. The world takes off its hat to those who put in more than 50% of their capacity, and stands on its head for those few and far between souls who devote 100%." - ANDREW CARNEGIE

"All our dreams can come true if we have the courage to pursue them." - WALT DISNEY

"For of those to whom much is given, much is required." - JOHN F KENNEDY

∞ Happiness and Peace ∞

In this section we will explore the keys to increasing the happiness and peace we experience in our lives. The two major keys deal with what you focus on and what type of perspective you have of your world. It can be confusing to grow up during the age of television when we are bombarded with graphic details of all the worlds ills and evils. Obviously, that is distorting our focus of how the world really is. Television and mass marketing may also play an important role in our lives regarding what our perspective of life is. Advertising teaches us that we cannot be happy unless we use the product featured in the ad. After all, how could anyone be happy without owning the world's finest automobile! Hopefully, you will find this section very refreshing as well as liberating of the materialistic mass media we are all exposed to.

Life becomes what you focus on; heaven and hell exist for each person, choose wisely what you focus on.

To discover what you truly value, think about what you will miss most once it is gone.

"The pain of leaving those you've grown to love is only the prelude to an understanding of yourself and others." - SHIRLEY MACLANE

As a young Marine officer, I spent long hours trying to learn all of the drills, inspecting the troops and barracks, working with the squad leaders and platoon sergeants, and developing training scenarios. I spent too many hours doing my job instead of living life. Then a wise and more mature officer pulled me aside after observing me for a few weeks. He asked me a question that I will never forget. "What will you miss most about your life once you are gone?" At first the question stumped me. But, as I began to ponder over it, I realized that I would miss the people I love, like my family and friends, walking underneath a starry sky during a peaceful night, and watching the sun set along a beautiful beach. I would not miss any of the material things in my life. My car, my house, my furniture, my clothes... I would only miss the essence of life itself... love, people, nature and the time to experience them. It then became obvious that a more balanced focus of career, relationships and nature contribute to a fulfilling life. What about you? What will you miss the most if you were to lose it tomorrow?

*What the mind often focuses on,
often comes to pass.*

*Your level of stress will be directly proportional to the
time it takes you to act on what ever worries you.*

*Faith gives you the ability to see through the down times
in life so you can make it to the good times.*

I was fortunate to enjoy the study of history growing up. I found it interesting to get a perspective of what daily life was like for the average person during different times of history. It is also fascinating to wonder what the daily life of some of the greatest kings and the richest people have been through out the years. As I thought about this, I came to a great realization. I have a much richer and fuller life than nearly any of the great kings or rich men who lived before the 20th century. Napoleon would loved to have owned a TV and to have been entertained by hundreds of movies, and to have seen events all over the world, and to have experienced all kinds of music and entertainment. Queen Elizabeth would have loved to have been able to drive in a car with a great stereo and air conditioning in great comfort over nice roads that have a variety of tasty restaurants. King Solomon would have loved to have been able to fly in a jet around the world, and George Washington would have loved to have taken care of his tooth ache by a modern dentist. We truly live better now as an average person than any of the richest people of the past. There has never been a better time to live than now. How's that for a great perspective on life!

Depression is the result of focussing only on your life instead of the lives of others.

A man becomes free by seeking responsibility for everything in his life, a man becomes a slave by rationalizing everything in his life.

Never lose touch of the needs of those you can help, for joy is close behind.

In today's world of TV and mass marketing, it can be easy to focus on the subtle messages that 'you're not good enough unless you drive this car' or 'you're not a success unless you wear these clothes' or 'you're not desirable unless you look like this model wearing this perfume'. Whheeewwww! No wonder so many people out there are depressed. You just can't buy everything advertised that is supposed to give you the 'feeling of success.' Many of us go deep into debt trying to. Instead, what would happen if we focussed on what we have to offer others. That might be healthier than focussing on what we can't give ourselves. True joy and satisfaction comes from helping others enjoy life. How does it feel when you help a loved one through a tough time and they acknowledge how much you mean to them? Our purpose in life is not to see how much we can acquire, but to see how much we can inspire! Who can you focus on today?

*The sooner we accept our limitations,
the sooner we overcome them.*

*The saddest thought is that
of what might have been.*

*To live a lie is slavery,
to live the truth is freedom and joy.*

When a person resists a limitation they possess, they give more weight and substance to their limitation. A man who worries about being smart enough may over compensate by trying to show that he does not need to study, telling people how smart he really is, speaking up on subjects which he knows very little, and boring people about the few things he may know. The more he pursues this path, the more the world will reflect to him how much intelligence he actually lacks. Once he accepts the fact that he needs to learn more, he will spend time reading, studying, listening to others, and learn more about the world and people around him. Once he takes this new course of action, he has started down the road to overcome his limitations. What limitations do you need to accept? Where can you begin to overcome your limitations? Even Aristotle said right before he died "All I know is that I know nothing." Perhaps the more you know, the more you realize what you don't know.

Hope is seeing one's purpose evolve, joy is seeing one's purpose fulfilled.

Once we realize that the mood of others has little to do with us, we can let go of the burden of taking everything personally.

Seeking the love and good in all people is the path to joy.

The world gets better when peacemakers attain greater respect than warriors.

Another lesson in the movie "It's A Wonderful Life" deals with the scene in the movie when George Bailey is a teenager working at the local drugstore. George is being his cheerful self serving customers in the store. His whistling gets on the nerves of the druggist. He yells "I'm not paying you to be a canary!" Obviously he is upset with George. Later on, George observes the druggist fumbling around with a presciption for a customer. It appears that the druggist messed up the ingredients. George tries to ask his dad what to do. His dad is in an important meeting. He does not deliver the prescription and by the time George gets back, the customer has called looking for their medicine. The druggist gets upset and slaps George across the head. Fortunately, young George Bailey did not take it personally because he saw a telegram that stated the death of the druggist's beloved son. George explained about what appeared to be a mistake in the mixing of the prescription. The druggist checked it out and discovered he almost poisoned his customer. When someone is upset, it often has little to do with you. When you get upset, make sure others know it has little to do with them!

*Guilt is the root of most disease,
forgiveness is the cure.*

To let go of control is to be in control.

*"Am I not destroying my enemies when
I make friends with them?"* - ABRAHAM LINCOLN

"The price of greatness is responsibility." - Winston Churchill

"Add up what you have, and you'll find that you won't sell them for all the gold in the world." - Dale Carnegie

"We can do no great things, only small things with great love." - Mother Teresa

∞ Success and Failure ∞

There are many ideas about what success is. People make numerous attempts at what often seems to be an illusionary goal. But all too often, we seem to easily attract different varieties of failure into our lives. What most people don't usually realize; more failure often relates in due time to more success. A very successful man was interviewed about what his secret to success was. He stated "good decisions." When further asked how he learned to make good decisions, he stated "through experience." When asked how he gained his experience, he stated "through making bad decisions." Often the mistakes we make are simply lessons we must learn so that we can make bigger and better things happen down the road. I hope you use this section to learn not to fear failure and to take action to go after your dreams and achieve success!

The greatest challenges mold the greatest men.

The more you are willing to hurt, fail and lose,
the more you will be able to love, succeed and win.

Increasing knowledge builds courage, building courage sparks
action, sparking action increases failure, increasing failure
builds experience, and building experience creates success.

Here is a great example of a man who overcame adversity to be a truly great leader. At the age of 23 his business failed. At age 24 he was defeated in a legislative race. At age 26 yet another business failed. At age 27 his sweetheart died. The combination of losing his mother as an infant, his sister at age 21, and his other adversities lead to a nervous breakdown at age 28. At age 30 he lost another election. At the ages of 35, 38 and 40 he lost congressional races. At age 47 he lost a senatorial race, at age 48 failed in an effort to become vice president, and at age 50 lost another senatorial race. Yet, at age 52, Abraham Lincoln became President of the United States. His leadership helped America through one of its greatest trials, the Civil War. He became known as one of the greatest leaders of modern history. Had he run from his challenges and adversities, what would have happened to the U.S. ? On top of his other problems, Lincoln suffered from the loss of two of his three children. How much adversity have you had to face? How has it helped you grow?

*Knowledge without action is worse
than action without knowledge.*

*Having a great idea does not equate to success;
acting on it before anyone else does equates to success.*

*"It is better to go after something great and fail,
than to attempt nothing and succeed."* - ROBERT SCHULLER

Henry Ford can arguably be considered one of the most successful men of the 20th century. He became one of the world's most powerful men by developing an automobile that was attainable by the masses. He used vision and hard work to develop the assembly line. He was responsible for creating many developments in manufacturing. One goal Ford had was to develop bullet proof glass. He approached the most knowledgeable experts in the field of glass. They all told him it would be impossible. Ford then hired a few personnel considered "lesser experts" in the field of glass. These people were not hindered with too much knowledge on what was not possible, but instead, sought to produce what was possible. They ran into many failures, but, eventually produced the bullet proof glass. Often, when we focus on our goal instead of our fear, the result is success. What "experts" are telling you that your dream can't work?

*From the pursuit of perfection
lies the birth of excellence.*

*The only true failure occurs when
the pursuit of a goal ends not accomplished.*

*"The world breaks all of us, but we grow stronger
in the broken places."* - ERNEST HEMINGWAY

A person may strive to run the fastest mile or to perform the most beautiful music on a piano. Through perfecting their body and mind, their performance improves. Through practice and exercise, the body and mind become one. Eventually, what once took great effort, now becomes effortless. Even though perfection may be impossible to truly attain, we find that we have attained excellence in the pursuit of perfection. We must always appreciate the growth we experience as we pursue perfection, even though we may never fully attain it. With this attitude, we can be at peace with not being perfect, and enjoy the excellence at anything we pursue in life. What do you wish to attain excellence in?

*Achievement is the combination
of concept and belief put into action.*

*It is amazing what you can accomplish when you don't care
about who gets the credit and the possibility of failing.*

*People will do more to avoid pain than to gain pleasure. A secret
in life is to do more to gain pleasure than to avoid pain.*

Beethoven is renowned as one of the greatest composers of all time. Yet he had to overcome his own obstacles and pain in order to create some of the worlds finest music. The combination of a strict father and the loneliness that often coincides with being a genius were a lot to bear for a young man. On top of this, one of his most important senses, the sense of hearing, began to diminish throughout his life. By the time Beethoven completed his 9th Symphony he was completely deaf. Beethoven focused on the pleasure of his music, not on the pain of his life and the limitations of his hearing. In his mind he could still hear his music. Because of his deafness and his genius, few people understood him. But God put a desire in Beethoven to create music. When Beethoven finally performed his 9th Symphony, the crowd in the concert hall clapped and yelled in delight to his music. However, he could not hear the applause. A member of the orchestra came to Beethoven and had him face the crowd so he could see their wild clapping and cheering faces. Beethoven was very moved to see that he had overcome his limitation and was still able to produce music that moved others. What do you want to accomplish?

*To focus on the positive of life is to see your world expand,
to focus on the negative of life is to see your world contract.*

*To increase your value, find a need to fill; to increase someone
else's value, show them a need that they already fill.*

*When you look for the child in everyone,
the world becomes a big playground.*

When I was a young Marine platoon commander, I spent time in Thailand working with the Thai Marines in the rural villages. These villages were composed of thatched huts along rice fields. The lives of the villagers were very simple. However, they knew that the American Marines were there to help protect their way of life. The people were very grateful and offered my men fruit, water, rice and anything else they had to offer. I was struck by the fact that they had very little, but offered whatever there was. They seemed very happy in their simple life with their family and loved ones. I reflected back to the United States where many people from prosperous backgrounds were depressed, dependant on drugs or alcohol, or had even attempted suicide. The villagers tended to focus on the family and joy of life, the Americans who were depressed seemed to focus on themselves and what they didn't have. You could make a case that the villagers were actually more successful than the "rich" Americans. How successful are you in defining what makes you rich in life?

*It is always better to under state and
deliver more than you promised.*

*Don't look at where someone comes from,
look at where they are going.*

*"If a man has done his best,
what else is there?"* - Gen. George S. Patton

Many people are waiting for everything in their life to be just right before they go after their dreams or goals. Most people don't realize that we are like a heat seeking rocket. If the only time you take off would be when your target comes directly overhead, you may never take off! However, even if the target is not straight overhead, you can take off anyway. Now, you are not going towards the target, but after making a few adjustments to your path, and following your heat seeking gyroscope(your desire), you are headed right at your target (your goal). So, eventually, after making a few corrections, you hit your target. In the mean time, the other rockets are still sitting on their launch pad waiting for their target to come directly overhead. Which kind of rocket are you? When will you take off toward your goals?

"It's hard to appreciate the magnificence from the highest mountaintops until you've been through the lowest valleys." - RICHARD NIXON

"In any moment of decision the best thing you can do is the right thing, the next best thing is the wrong thing, and the worst thing you can do is nothing." - THEODORE ROOSEVELT

"The quality of a persons life is in direct proportion to their commitment to excellence, regardless of their chosen field of endeavor." - VINCE LOMBARDI

"The only limit to our realization of tomorrow will be our doubts of today." - FRANKLIN D. ROOSEVELT

Try to imagine being very successful and then having everything stripped away from you. That is exactly what happened to Viktor Frankl. He wrote about his experiences surviving the Nazi concentration camp at Auschwitz in his book "Man's Search For Meaning." He describes how his home and possessions were confiscated, and how his father, mother, brother and wife went up in ashes or died in camp. Most of us find it difficult at times to keep focussed on success. Frankl was able to survive tremendous hunger, humiliation, and pain because he developed meaning from his suffering. He made it his purpose in life to survive the camp so he could tell the world and keep this type of butchery from happening to future generations. One of Frankl's favorite quotes is by Nietzche "He who has a why to live can bear with almost any how." If a man can find meaning and purpose in a concentration camp, what meaning and purpose can you find where you are? Once you discover your purpose in life, you discover understanding and the strength to pursue that purpose. When you can answer - what am I good at, how can I contribute to others, and what is my heart's desire - your purpose is not far behind.

∽ MENTAL, PHYSICAL AND SPIRITUAL ∽

This section is intended to help you take a look at who you are and what you are. Every person is a makeup of mental, physical and spiritual. Some philosophers have stated "Mind, body and soul." To have a fulfilling life, it is important to develop in each of these areas. We can view these three areas like spokes on a wheel. If you are strong mentally, weak physically, and average spiritually, your life will be a little lopsided. Eventually, your health will diminish and your brain will lose it's mental edge because of the reduced blood flow and oxygen to it. If you are strong mentally and physically, but weak spiritually, you will fill an emptiness at times from lack of purpose or faith. All three areas support each other. The stronger you become in each area, the farther your wheel can take you. The bigger your wheel, the easier you can get over life's obstacles.

*Becoming aware of the miracles around us
is the beginning of a true appreciation for life.*

*Knowledge begins with the fear of God, life begins with the love
of God, peace begins with the will of God, and faith begins
with the experience of God.*

*Live today as if not only your life depended on it,
but also all eternity.*

In my youth I watched an interview with the Pope. The Pope was asked "If you were to die tomorrow and find there was no God, would you have wasted your life serving something that did not exist?" The Pope simply replied "If you were to die tomorrow and find out that there really was a God, could you have wasted eternity by not serving a God who actually did exist?" Pursuing a path of spiritual growth obviously has its advantages. Thomas Jefferson stated "Of all the systems of morality, ancient or modern, which have come under my observation, none appears to me so pure as that of Jesus." It is up to each person to follow their heart when it comes to God. It has been stated that George Washington, Abraham Lincoln and Franklin Roosevelt spent many moments in prayer when faced with the difficulties of being president during tough times. How much easier could you face adversity if you had a greater spiritual reserve?

*The more man develops science and knowledge,
the more science and knowledge reveals God.*

"Called or not called, God is present." - CARL JUNG

*Life is simple - the world reflects back how our soul is doing.
The weight of your burdens are inversely proportional to
your faith in God.*

It is amazing to discover that as mankind has developed awareness of his universe that the proof of God develops along with it. A first case in point is the fact that with man's knowledge of science, organic chemistry, biology and life, he is finding it nearly impossible to see how inorganic chemicals in our universe randomly came together to form life. If life could occur randomly, scientists should have been able to create life on their own by taking these same chemicals and mixing them together. A second case in point is a discovery noted by Stephen Hawking in his book "A Brief History Of Time." He states that by using the Doppler effect to observe the universe, astronomers can determine if stars in the universe are moving towards us or away from us. They discovered that all stars are moving away from us at the same exact rate. The only way this is possible is if we are at the center of the universe which is expanding. Hawking demonstrates that the mathematical odds of being in the center are mind boggling and lead one to consider the real possibility of God. Is it just a coincidence that we are at the center of the universe?

*Spiritual, the more you seek it the higher you go;
material, the more you seek it the lower you fall.*

*"I have lived, Sir, a long time, and the longer I live, the more
convincing proofs I see of this truth - that God governs
in the affairs of men."* - BENJAMIN FRANKLIN

*"Not he is great who can alter matter, but he who can alter my
state of mind."* - RALPH WALDO EMERSON

John F. Kennedy stated "This country cannot afford to be materially rich and spiritually poor." When I review the lives of some of the world's greatest people, I find that all of them have one key similarity. They all proclaimed a strong faith in God. I have found that my faith has given me the enthusiasm and will to live life to the fullest. It has given me a feeling of purpose. When you truly evaluate your life, you discover that without purpose, you are merely existing. I have simply sought out the people, both present and past, whom I most admire and tried to emulate them. Through this pursuit, much like Benjamin Franklin, I have found more evidence of the presence of God. What miracles are going on around you at this very minute? What can you do to increase your awareness of God? Do the people you respect and admire have spiritual depth?

Knowledge is the leverage of life.

Your attitude plus aptitude equals your altitude.

"If a man empties his purse into his head no one can take it away from him. An investment in knowledge always pays the best interest." - BENJAMIN FRANKLIN

Many success authors have expressed that positive thinking, enthusiasm and a great attitude are important to success. This is true. But it is only a part of the equation. A very strong man with a great deal of enthusiasm and an incredible attitude may still have a difficult, if not impossible time, moving a huge bolder. However, with a knowledge of physics, he can move a small rock next to the bolder and use it as a fulcrum. He can then grab a sturdy pole and leverage his strength and weight to move the bolder. This is a good analogy on how life is. Man, with all the enthusiasm and belief in the world, still can't jump off a building and fly. With the development of man's knowledge, we have built aircraft that can take us anywhere we want to go. We are very fortunate to live in an age where the combination of our knowledge and enthusiasm can equate to nearly anything. What can you accomplish with a little enthusiasm and know how?

How you maintain yourself physically reflects how you feel mentally; how you maintain yourself mentally effects how you feel physically.

Pain can be like the weeds in a garden; the sooner you get rid of them, the less problems they cause you down the road.

It is more true to state "as a man thinks, then does, he is." Thinking without action is useless.

Medicine and science are revealing how powerful our mental state is regarding health. One of the most inspiring stories I know about is that of Norman Cousins. He was diagnosed with a severe form of cancer and was given slim odds of recovery. He decided to watch movies and read books that made him laugh a lot. By keeping a great attitude and a determination to live, Norman fully recovered. He writes about his experience in the book "Anatomy of an Illness." By laughing a lot we can strengthen the immune system by deeper breathing, increased lymphatic stimulation, and an overall feeling of energy and liveliness. Many books talk of the importance of breathing in regard to health. I fully believe that any activity we do to increase the volume and pace of breathing is great for our longevity. Exercising, yoga, and just pure fun are good for the body and the soul. Stress tends to cause rapid, weak, and shallow breathing. When we don't get enough oxygen to our cells, disease is the result. What can you do today to put deep, healthy breathing back into your life?

It is natural for lust to attract us to someone - much like animals in nature - it is our mind and soul which allow us to go beyond lust to love.

"The weak can never forgive - forgiveness is the attribute of the strong." - MAHATMA GANDHI

"Give a man a fish and you feed him for a day. Teach a man to fish and you feed him for a lifetime." - CHINESE PROVERB

One of the keys to having a happy and prosperous life is to find a spouse that we are compatible with on a mental, spiritual, and physical level. We are by nature attracted to many different people based solely on physical chemistry. We are often attracted to people who appear to be most like ourselves. Many people have made the mistake of looking for someone they find only physically attractive to try to form a lifetime relationship with. This relationship will be exciting at first, but will require the other two key elements to survive the trials and tribulations of everyday life together. It is important to find someone with whom you are compatible both mentally and spiritually. As we age, these two elements become increasingly important. Having someone that you gain emotional support from, as well as share basic values, ideas, and dreams with, will take you a long way. Finding someone who you are compatible with on all three levels is key to a great life long relationship!

∞ BALANCE AND GROWTH ∞

This section addresses two key elements to be aware of constantly in life. It is important to maintain balance and growth. When you lose balance, the synergy of your life will begin to weaken. A good analogy is a chain of many links. If each link has roughly the same strength (is balanced), then each link pulls its share of the weight. However, if one or two of the links are rusting, then disaster may be close at hand. When your growth slows or even ends all together, you will develop a state of lethargy, stagnation or even have life diminish. Each and every day you are either putting effort into making your life better, or your life is beginning to lessen instead. Nothing in life stays constant, you are either getting better or worse. When a man exercises, stretches, eats right, and maintains his body, he becomes healthier. When he is lazy, smokes, eats junk food, and watches TV all of the time, he encourages weakness. To continue to grow mentally, physically and spiritually with balance in each area is a key to life.

All life is a perfect balance, therefore consider the reverse image of what you see to insure that you gain a more complete picture.

To understand something, a person must first seek many viewpoints, give each a chance, see what results, and then when a new viewpoint appears; start over.

The first step of knowledge begins with recognizing what you don't know; the more you learn, the more you realize how much you don't know.

Dying begins when growth ends.

Thomas Edison is known as one of the greatest inventors of all times. He demonstrated a continued zeal to create, gain knowledge, experiment, and develop inventions to serve mankind. He is probably most famous for the development of the light bulb. Edison was asked if it was a waste of time and a lot of frustration with all of the failures he experienced trying to create the light bulb. He simply stated that he had discovered 1,800 ways of how not to make a light bulb. Eventually, after testing hundreds of filaments, Edison discovered that the filament which lasted the longest would work well in a vacuum. He realized that in a vacuum the filament could not oxidize, therefore, the light would last. What areas of life are you ready to grow in? What kind of experiments can you begin?

*Everything happens in cycles; when times are good, prepare for
the bad; when times are bad, look forward to the good.*

*If everything is going smoothly,
you must not be pushing yourself.*

*Since we learn from our mistakes, life becomes easier
with the more mistakes we overcome.*

*Seek a few who can help you grow,
then allow others to seek you to help them grow.*

One of the very first inspirational books I ever read was "How To Win Friends And Influence People" by Dale Carnegie. The next book I read was "Think And Grow Rich" by Napoleon Hill. Both of these men took life seriously. Each sought out men of success to determine what they could learn from them to become successful themselves. Even more importantly, these two men took the knowledge they acquired and wrote their books which have influenced and motivated thousands, if not millions, of people over the last two generations. Throughout their lives they continued on their search to find more information that would contribute to helping others get more out of life. If you were to push yourself and seek those who could help you grow, what could you do in life?

On their deathbed no one ever says
"I wish I would have spent more time with my job."

If you are satisfied with your life the way it is,
maintain your level of mental, physical and spiritual being.
If you aren't satisfied, increase your levels.

It is much more enjoyable in life to start at a lower place
and end up higher, than to start at a higher place and end up
lower. Seeing growth in life is satisfying. Be thankful for your
simple beginning. Most great people have came from
humble stations in life.

"If there is no struggle, there is no progress." - Frederick Douglas

There are often many illusions regarding successful people. Some of these illusions are that "she was lucky," "he was given everything," "everything comes easy for him," "they were born into the right family," etc... In truth, most of the successful people I have studied actually overcame a great deal of adversity and experienced a lot of growth to get where they are. Alex Haley's book "Roots" took years of development and frustration before it finally became a hit TV series. Many successful people also come from very simple, if not challenging backgrounds. My father dropped out of school after the 8th grade. He joined the Navy at the age of 17 and married my mother at 19. Coming from this simple and humble background, I have still been able to achieve many of my dreams. I have had many opportunities in my life. Even so, I had to be ready to grab them. Working summers and with help from the Marine Corps, I became the first of my relatives to earn a college degree. I am excited when I look back on life and recognize lots of growth from my experiences, as well as a good balance between a career I enjoy and the people I love. What is helping you grow? How is life preparing you for success?

"The unexamined life is not worth living" - SOCRATES

"There is a fine balance to humility and pride; try to be overly humble or prideful and you cause the contrary, be slightly humble of your station in life and respect will follow."
- BALTASAR GRACIAN

*"Two roads diverged in a wood,
and I took the one less traveled by,
and that has made all the difference."* - ROBERT FROST

"Anyone who stops learning is old, whether at twenty or eighty. Anyone who keeps learning stays young." - HENRY FORD

We all must sit down and take a look at our lives every now and then. We often reflect back on things when we experience loss, heartache or failure. I learned a very big lesson while I was in the Aggie Band at Texas A&M. I had become very successful as a cadet. I had attained a high rank and would hold a commanding officer position my senior year. I had become a member of the Ross Volunteers honor company. I had attained a lot of honors and awards. I was very satisfied and very proud. The only honor left was to be part of the front rank of the band reserved for seniors who possessed the best marching and leadership skills. These seniors are selected by the drum majors. I assumed that since I held one of the top positions in the band and I had excelled in Best Drilled competition that I was a shoe in. However, I was about to get a lesson in both politics and humility. When the selections for Bugle Rank(the front rank) were announced, I was not among the seniors selected. After a lot of tears, pain and searching, I discovered that my perception of success had lead a 20-year-old to arrogance. This alienated the drum majors and influenced their choices. I learned the importance of humility, teamwork, and influence. I more importantly learned no matter how successful you are(or think you are) that there is always a lot to learn, and you can never stop growing.

∽ Problems and Solutions ∽

We all realize that each of us has to face his or her share of problems in life. The good news is that problems bring with them the seeds of their own solutions as well as the seeds of a more fulfilling life. John F. Kennedy noted once that the Chinese symbol for crisis is also the same symbol for opportunity. This makes a good point that whether a situation is seen as a problem or an opportunity depends on how you perceive it. Most people simply want to avoid problems and live in security. However, the only ones with no problems are the ones buried in cemeteries. Helen Keller stated it best as "Security is mostly superstition. It does not exist in nature... Life is either a daring adventure or nothing." Let's take a look on how we can use our own problems and their solutions to make our life an adventure!

*Life begins to require less effort once you accept
the fact that life will always be an effort.*

*Once you accept that life will always have its share
of difficulties, you will be able to enjoy it when it doesn't.*

*Problems are usually not far behind when we
put off what needs to be done today.*

Too many people know and love the story of Cinderella and Prince Charming. They meet at the ball with the help of the Fairy Godmother, fall in love, and live happily ever after. This has lead many people to believe that once they get that perfect job, the fine automobile, the beautiful house, the right mate, that incredible... that they too will live happily ever after. Remember... Cinderella was a make believe fairy tale! What we are living is called "Real Life"! With enough experience in life, we can reflect back on different things we have attained which we thought would make us happy. I remember getting my dream house. It was perfect until I became a slave to the house by working to pay for it and working to take care of it. As I looked back on my life, I realized that I was no more happier in that home than when I was living in the officer barracks in Quantico, Virginia as a lieutenant barely making over $1,000 per month. We don't need to wait until we get everything we want, and have no more problems, to be happy. All we need to do is appreciate our friends and life as we go along. Besides, the only people who don't have problems are six feet under in the cemetery.

Find an uncommon challenge for all to focus on and then you have the power to unite an uncommon people.

God does not give us the desire for something without providing the ability for us to attain it, nor does God provide a challenge without a way to meet it.

The improvements you make in yourself are directly proportional to the improvements you will see in your world.

I noticed an interesting principle of life when I went overseas in the Marine Corps with my platoon. While we were in California at Camp Pendleton, my men existed in small clicks based on race or religion or other like interests. When we were in Asia, we all became the minority. We were now Americans. Everyone got along great. After seeing our camaraderie grow, it became my wish that everyone would see themselves as citizens of the world and mankind! A special man exemplified rising to an "uncommon challenge" during the 1960's in America. He was Martin Luther King, Jr. He stood up for the rights of all men and demonstrated that through love of fellow man and peaceful demonstration, that right really does make might. King made one of America's most courageous and inspiring speeches the day before he was assassinated in Memphis, Tennessee. "...We've got difficult days ahead. But it really doesn't matter to me now. Because I've been to the mountaintop!... Like anybody, I would like to live a long life, but I'm not concerned about that now. I just want to do God's will. And he has allowed me to go up to the mountain and I've seen the Promised Land. I may not get there with you, but I want you to know tonight, that we as a people will get to the Promised Land!" What is your challenge?

Man attracts into his life what is needed for his soul's growth and wonders why there is so much struggle trying to attain the things of the world.

To criticize a problem can only be done if a solution has been found, should only be of the item and not the person, should contain your humanness and empathy, should be done one on one where there is no shame but encouragement to do better in the future.

To worry or criticize what you can't change is simply wasted living.

Winston Churchill is another historical figure of great magnitude who lead England through some of her darkest hours during World War II. Few people realize the difficulties that Churchill had to overcome in his youth. As a young man, he had difficulty speaking because of a pronounced stutter. He also was a poor student. He had to take an exam twice to barely get into a military academy. His problems became a hidden blessing when he discovered an understanding of the English language. As he studied English, his confidence grew and he became more comfortable with speaking. Once he overcame his stuttering, speaking became even a greater joy. The rest is history. Often, history has demonstrated that people with severe handicaps have utilized their afflictions to launch them to greater heights. Even John F. Kennedy used his time recovering from a back injury to write his Pulitzer Prize winning book "Profiles of Courage." What problems do you have that can help you grow?

"The only thing necessary for the triumph of evil is for good men to do nothing." - EDMUND BURKE

"In the middle of difficulty lies opportunity." - ALBERT EINSTEIN

"Hate the sin and love the sinner." - MAHATMA GANDHI

"There is no education like adversity." - BENJAMIN DISRAELI

Problems, adversity, and difficulties plague all of us. However, once we overcome them, our life is usually more enriched. A good example is learning to snow ski. Over and over I had to overcome the problem of how to stop while going downhill. I had to negotiate the difficulty of maintaining my balance as I ran over bumps. I had to conquer the adversity of falling, getting my skis back, and then getting right back up again. Eventually, with the help of others and persistence from myself, skiing became really enjoyable. I saw skiing like life. The sooner you get out there and learn to overcome different problems, adversities, difficulties, and obstacles; the sooner you learn how to handle them the next time around. The sooner you also are able to enjoy the greater adventures in life as well! Imagine if we were all given a quota of problems we each had to solve before life would be fulfilling. The best thing to do, is try to work through them as soon as possible so you can enjoy the 'ski slopes of life'!

∞ LOVE AND FEAR ∞

No one can have a fulfilling life without living in the presence of love. The opposite of living in the presence of love is living in fear. Ignorance, hate, judgment and blame are all intertwined with a life of fear. Knowledge, joy, acceptance, and forgiveness are aspects of a life in the presence of love. The more we increase our knowledge, joy, acceptance and forgiveness of others, the more we will experience love and the less we will experience fear. This can be considered the most important section of this book. If you have love and have nothing else you are still a rich person. If you have all the riches in the world and have no love, you are mute. It is my sincerest desire that this section will help you become more aware of how to increase love and decrease fear in your life.

*Look for the love in others and
that is what they will find in you.*

*Each person has a special way of experiencing and giving love;
learn this and your ability to experience and give love
to others will magnify.*

*Anyone can love those who love them, to make the world
better, we must learn to love all the rest.*

*The key to making the world better is discovering how much
love there is and then showing everyone.*

In my search for a fuller life, I participated in different seminars, workshops and events. In 1991 I participated in a weekend workshop called "Return to the Heart" by Bill Ferguson. I credit a great deal of my understanding of love to the Bible and to the work Bill put together. During this weekend I made many dramatic realizations. One was through observing a couple who was participating due to marriage difficulties. They had been married over seven years and each felt that they were not getting the love they needed from each other. Bill asked what made each of them feel really loved as a child. The husband said that when he received a present, he felt loved. His wife stated that when she was told how pretty she was, or received a compliment, she felt loved. It was like a light went on for the couple and everyone in the group. We all realized what the problem was. He had been giving her love the way he experienced it, by gifts. She had been giving him love the way she experienced it, by giving him compliments. Neither experienced love that way. Once they realized what made the other feel loved, they were able to recognize the love they had been receiving all along, and more importantly, they are now able to give their partner what made them feel most loved. What makes your special person feel loved?

Acceptance and forgiveness are the building blocks of love.

Once you know yourself, love for everyone else should be easy.

To look at the worst in the world and accept that these are a part of you is a key to being able to accept and love everyone else.

To understand begins with first seeing our imperfections, and how we are unworthy, then to see how others are worth loving, then how God can love us, and finally we can see how to love ourselves.

As I have grown to know myself, I see all of the bad sides which exist opposite of my good sides. To know yourself is to accept the bad with the good. Once you accept the times when you feel anger, or lust for something that others have, or experience your bouts of selfishness; then you can show understanding of the human weakness that exists in others. It has been stated "There except for the grace of God go I." In other words, if I had been through the same things that poor soul had been through, it might be me. To know and love yourself is greatly related to your ability to understand and love others. I have become aware that as I grow to know and love myself more, I find it easier to understand and love others more. I believe you will discover that the more you help others feel accepted and loved, the more love and acceptance you will experience in life.

Increasing knowledge decreases fear.

To know everything is to fear nothing.

To live fully, is to pursue love and conquer fear.

When you encounter fear; look back on your life when you had a greater fear and then overcame it with knowledge and experience. Then you can realize that a few years from now that you will look on this current fear the same way.

Jesus worked hard to try to instill love and courage into his 12 disciples. However, because the disciples did not have the knowledge and understanding of Jesus, they still experienced a lot of fear. Jesus tried to explain to the disciples that they were wasting effort by fretting about everything. He used the example of the sparrow and how God took care of it's needs. Since people are more important to God than sparrows, how much more will God address our needs. The greatest fear the disciples experienced occurred when their leader, Jesus, was arrested and taken away. Their fear was so great because the person they looked up to and believed in was so easily taken. The disciples were ignorant of God's purpose with Jesus. However, history notes that 11 of the 12 disciples faced enormous adversity and died tragic deaths. What made these cowards become so courageous? Once Jesus was crucified, the disciples remained hidden from authorities. Three days later, the spirit of Jesus appeared to the disciples giving them understanding and faith in God's power over death and the world. With the knowledge and experience the disciples gained from the risen Jesus, nearly all fear subsided. The New Testament records the rest. What fear can you conquer with knowledge?

*The greatest opportunity for growth lies in
overcoming what you fear.*

*The greatest pain we experience will be the love we take to our
death that we should have given while we were living.*

*Our ability to live and love is directly related to our ability
to experience and let go of pain.*

*To accept our own death is to accept the preciousness
of each and every moment of life.*

When I was in the Marine Corps at Camp Pendleton, I ran across a newspaper story that was very moving. It was so inspirational that I shared it with my men. The story covered the experiences of some of the soldiers who fought in the Normandy invasion during World War II. Many of the men experienced fears of never seeing their loved ones again as well as if they or their buddy next to them would survive battle. Many brave souls did perish in the invasion and many families lost loved ones. After the invasion was successful, some of the men began to return back to the U.S. The boat trip back home took a few days and gave all of the soldiers who survived time to reflect on their experiences and the life they now cherished more than ever. The story ends by describing how moved these tough men were when they came into New York harbor and saw the Statue of Liberty as bands played "God Bless America." Every man on that boat dropped to his knees, and with tremendous emotion and tears, gave thanks to God up above for their life, their families, and their country. What can we do to appreciate the life we have? What fears do you have that keep you from living life?

All the darkness of the universe can't hide a single point of light.

Love is directly proportional to the level of sacrifice you are willing to give.

Prejudice is the by-product of ignorance.

What a wonderful world it will be when we each see skin color as we do the color of roses; they are all beautiful.

Prejudice broken down into two words is "pre judge." When we make judgment of someone based on a small amount of information, we are showing prejudice. We are fortunate to exist in a country and time where knowledge and awareness is minimizing prejudices. There are examples of many great Americans, as well as World Leaders, from every race, creed, sex and origin. It is wise for us all to focus on the contributions that each group has given the World. We need to look for the love and greatness in everyone we meet. The more we learn and experience other cultures and people, the more love and the less fear we experience with them. My love and respect for Asian people grew from my experience overseas in the Marine Corps. A good example of someone being pre-judged regards a scrawny, freckle faced, kid who was in the Army in World War II. None of the drill sergeants felt he would amount to much. He seemed too shy and introverted to ever be much of a leader. Yet there he was. This young man became the most decorated hero of the war. His name was Audie Murphy. He held off a entire company of German troops from the top of a burning tank with a machine gun while his men regrouped. You just never know who the next hero might be! How can you be a hero?

"Darkness cannot drive out darkness; only light can do that. Hate cannot drive out hate; only love can do that." - MARTIN LUTHER KING, JR.

"Hatred can only be overcome by love." - MAHATMA GANDHI

"He who lives in fear will never, in my judgment, be a free man" - VIRGIL

"Let us endeavor so to live that when we come to die, even the undertaker will be sorry." - MARK TWAIN

I want to end this book with a story that conveys how important it is for each of us to communicate to the people we care about regarding the love we feel for them. Too often in life we recognize the love we should have demonstrated towards someone after it is too late. Many times this is realized after someone cherished leaves you, or after someone we love dies unexpectedly. I heard a story regarding a girl who lived in my hometown when I was in high school. Her parents were people who worked hard for everything they had. They had never owned a new automobile before. After having the car for a couple of weeks, her mom asked her to get a few things from the store. Her mom was too busy preparing for the evening so she was told to take the car to store and come back home when she was done. The excitement of driving the new car for the first time was nearly overwhelming. She met some friends along the way and went for a supposedly short joy ride. The joy ride ended when she ran the car into a ditch. Her fear rose as she recovered in the emergency room wondering what her parents would do. When her parents arrived, she was prepared for the worst. Instead, with tears in their eyes, her parents kissed and loved her. It was that day a teenage girl realized how much she was loved. Does everyone you care about really know how much you love them?

∞ My Formula for a Rich and Fulfilling Life ∞

W *Wake up to your purpose in life*
A *Appreciating your world and your life you have been given*
L *Love, developing love for yourself and for others*
K *Knowledge, developing it to make life more effortless and rewarding*

If you develop all four areas of this formula for your life, you will be able to **"WALK"** with ease through out life when many people are only crawling! After all, Jack London said "man's purpose is to live, not exist."

⁂ Ending Note ⁂

At no time in history has the ordinary person had so many opportunities to live a very fulfilling life. It is very important that you discover what your gift to the world is. Then it is just as important to use your gift to serve the world in which you live. I once heard that in every millionaire's home you will find a library. I started my library while in the Marine Corps and will never finish adding to it. Hopefully this book has sparked the desire to learn and understand more about life. On the following page is a list of books which have helped me a great deal and can give your further inspiration to getting everything you want from life!

∞ Sources of My Inspiration ∞

The Bible

Think and Grow Rich

Unlimited Power

The Seven Spiritual Laws of Success

The Power of Positive Thinking

How to Win Friends and Influence People

Wealth 101

Top Performance

Mans Search for Meaning

Men are From Mars, Women are From Venus

Bridge Across Forever

Zapp, The Lightning of Empowerment

∾ SOURCES OF MY INSPIRATION ∾

Even Eagles Need a Push

The One Minute Manager

Secrets from Great Minds

The Book of Virtues

The Winner Within

Miracles Are Guaranteed

Psychocybernetics

The University of Success

Ageless Body, Timeless Minds

The Seven Habits of Highly Effective People

Your Greatest Power

Closer to The Light

∞ A Request ∞

I have been asked to produce *The Courage Book*, and I need your help. I need real life stories about anyone who has overcome adversity and demonstrated courage to make the world better – please send your story to: Tim Gaither, Awaken Publishing
c/o Brockton Publishing Company
8326 Southwest Freeway
Houston, Texas 77074

Or you can fax it to (713) 771-6849.

Be sure to include your address and phone so I can contact you to discuss the possibility of including your story in *The Courage Book.*

∞ TO ORDER MORE COPIES ∞

Make a copy of this page and send it to us or call 1-800-968-7065

Awaken Publishing

c/o Brockton Publishing Company
8326 Southwest Freeway
Houston, Texas 77074

(713) 268-7065
Fax (713) 771-6849
1-800-968-7065

Name _____

Address _____

City, State, Zip _____

Phone _____

Send your order to: _____

☐ Check box if you have written special instructions on back of form.

The Inspiration Book is $9.95 plus $5.00 shipping & handling per book.
Orders will be shipped UPS to a street address only (Not a P.O. Box).
Texas residents, please add Texas sales tax of 8 1/4%.
I would like_____ copy(s) of *The Inspiration Book*.
Make checks payable to **Awaken Publishing** or you may charge your order to Visa, M.C. or American Express.

Card No. _____ Exp. Date _____